# Easter A to Z

## Victoria Fletcher

copyright © 2022 Victoria Fletcher
ISBN: 978-1-959700-01-2

Victoria Fletcher
hootbookspublishing.biz
vfletcher56@gmail.com

**A** is for the angel that came to
where the disciples stood looking up to the sky.
Jesus has ascended into heaven
and is in His place on high.

**B** is for betrayal
by one of His very own.
But it was part of the plan
that God would soon make known.

C is for the crown of thorns
pressed down on Jesus' head
when they crucified Him on the cross
because He took our place instead.

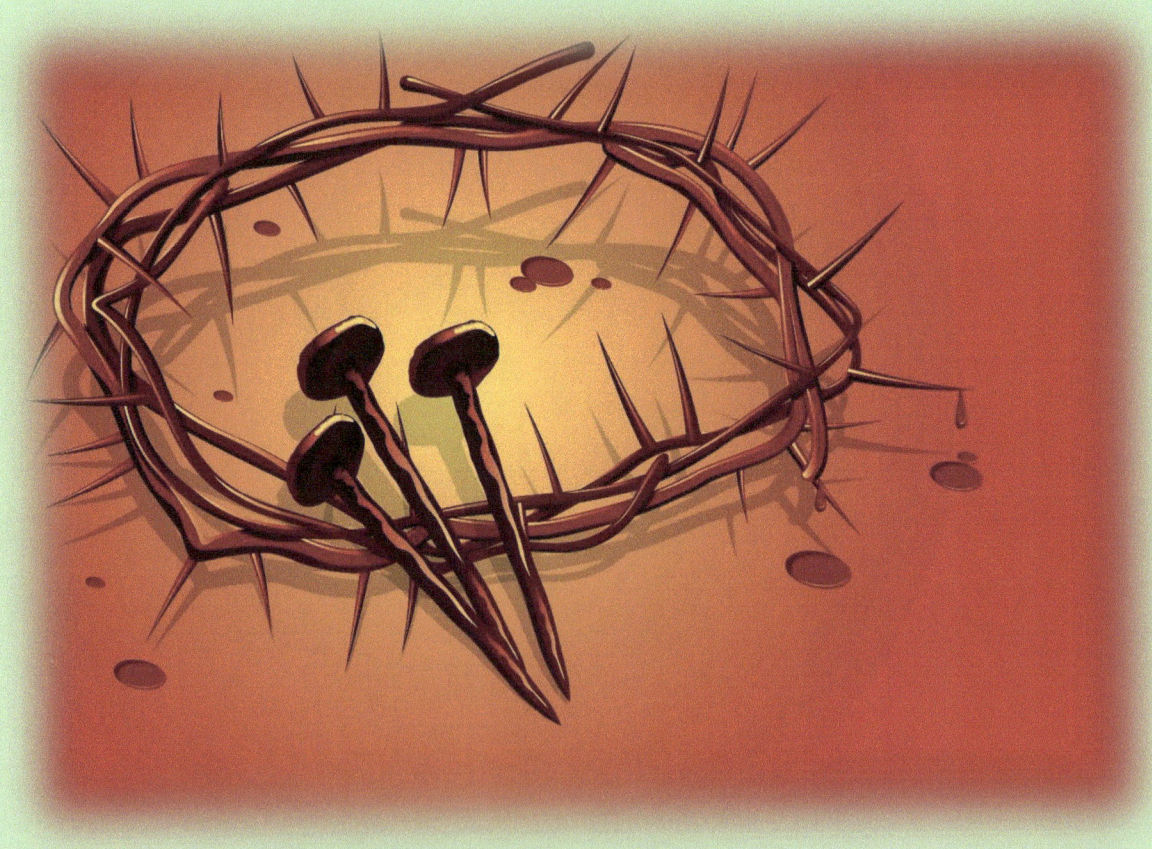

**D** is for denial.
Peter was sorry when the rooster crowed.
After Jesus died on the cross,
Peter remembered and his tears flowed.

**E** is for earthquake
that came when Jesus died.
The veil in the temple tore into
the day He was crucified.

**F** is for Father
whom Jesus called out to,
"Why have You forsaken Me?"
But He knew God's plan for you.

**G** is for the Garden of Gethsemane
where Jesus went to pray.
He found His disciples sleeping
but He told them it was okay.

**H** is for Hosanna in the Highest.
The people shouted this as He came.
Waving palm branches before Him
as they praised His holy name.

I is for "It is finished."
Jesus spoke these words before He died.
His mother Mary and many others
gathered together there and cried.

J is for Jesus, the Son of God,
who came to save us from sin.
If we believe He is God's Son,
we will one day live in heaven.

**K** is for the kiss when Judas betrayed the Lord.
Satan had filled Judas' heart.
Judas bargained for just thirty pieces of silver
and very soon regretted his part.

**L** is for the Lord's Supper,
the last meal before Jesus would be crucified.
He used this time to serve His disciples:
bread as His body and His blood was the wine.

**M** is for Mary, the mother of Jesus
and a follower named Mary Magdalene.
They watched as Jesus was hung on the cross.
They both cried at the death of the Son.

**N** is for the nail-scarred hands
Jesus showed to Thomas so he could believe.
Thomas did believe but Jesus said
that faith is believing without having seen.

**O** is for our command
to tell others about God's Son.
We are commanded to share the Good News
to each and every one.

**P** is for Pilate
who heard the case against Jesus.
Pilate told the people that he wanted no part
and he washed his hands of this.

**Q** is for questions
the chief priests asked, the hows and whys.
They tried to trick Jesus into saying something wrong
so they had cause for Him to die.

**R** is for resurrection,
the greatest part of the Easter story.
The grave could not hold our Lord.
God raised Him to save you and me.

**S** is for salvation,
the very reason Jesus died.
To save us from a sin-filled life
so one day in heaven we will abide.

**T** is for tomb
where Jesus' body was placed that day.
The tomb was empty when
they rolled the stone away.

**U** is for ultimate sacrifice.
Jesus gave His life for you and me.
God's plan to save His people
died on a cross at Calvary.

**V** is for victory.
Jesus rose from the grave.
God's Son brought us salvation.
Those who believe in Him will be saved.

**W** is for world.
God loves each and every one.
If we believe in Jesus,
we will someday live with God and His Son.

**X** is for χριστός (Christos)
which is Christ in Greek.
One of the words on the sign
hung above Jesus on that tree.

**Y** is for You!!!
The reason Jesus went to the grave.
God's love for all made Him decide,
His Son was the only way we could be saved.

**Z** is for Zacharias and his wife Elizabeth. The angel said their son would share the Word. John the Baptist was sent to prepare the way so Jesus would be known as Messiah and Lord.

www.ingramcontent.com/pod-product-compliance
Lightning Source LLC
Chambersburg PA
CBHW042126040426
42450CB00002B/92